T0004314

Forever My Dove

second edition

Ron Dailey

Illustrations by Neal Benge

TATE PUBLISHING
AND ENTERPRISES, LLC

Forever My Dove
Copyright © 2014 by Ron Dailey. All rights reserved.

No part of this publication may be reproduced, stored in a retrieval system or transmitted in any way by any means, electronic, mechanical, photocopy, recording or otherwise without the prior permission of the author except as provided by USA copyright law.

The opinions expressed by the author are not necessarily those of Tate Publishing, LLC.

Published by Tate Publishing & Enterprises, LLC
127 E. Trade Center Terrace | Mustang, Oklahoma 73064 USA
1.888.361.9473 | www.tatepublishing.com

Tate Publishing is committed to excellence in the publishing industry. The company reflects the philosophy established by the founders, based on Psalm 68:11,
"The Lord gave the word and great was the company of those who published it."

Book copyright © 2014 by Tate Publishing, LLC. All rights reserved.

Published in the United States of America

ISBN: 978-1-63449-561-5
Poetry / General
14.03.05

Forever My Dove

"There are some experiences in life that are just too rich to put into words. However, while unfolding the Story of Forever My Dove, I have tried earnestly to relate friendship and love at its best. I have felt love and friendship in its highest form, and many of my poems have come with a gift of tears. The very first piece of poetry I had ever written had a dove in it, and it was about love. It is from this first poem that Forever My Dove was borne. I hope you will treasure it always."
Ron Dailey/Author

"I recall as a child being very sick from scarlet fever. This sickness kept me in bed for several months. One very special memory during this time, was being awakened each morning by a beautiful cardinal. This bird would land on my windowsill, and stay until my mother would come into the room. I still remember the feelings that I had when I was visited by God's little pet. Even to this day, when I paint wildlife, I escape to those moments on the windowsill."
Neal Benge/Artist

To My Beloved _____
Gifted by _____

On the _____ Day of _____

Event _____

Personal Message: _____
_____
_____
_____
_____

Contents

Acknowledgements

I would like to thank Tom Mallets for his ingenious computer skills, Terry Wilson for his photography on page 3, Jack McKeen for final proofing, Neal Benge for everything, Lindsey Dailey, my daughter, for being my angel, Carole, my loving wife, and…, and a special thanks to my wonderful mother, for teaching me as a small child, how to love unconditionally.

Additional thanks goes to White Feather and Sweetie bird, my subjects, whom I will set free in the spring.

Preface

FOREVER MY DOVE is a most unique and extraordinary collection of Loveletters and Lovepoems. Prior to publishing, I did a survey in my hometown, and college campuses, and found that this collection had the strange capacity of making ladies cry, and arousing goosebumps on their arms.

This collection also had a similar effect on the opposite sex, and usually they would ask if they could purchase individual pages for their sweethearts.

I see FOREVER MY DOVE being purchased as the ideal wedding present, valentine's present, or a present for a friend or sweetheart. To this end, no expense has been spared. All the writings and paintings are original, and inspiring to each other.

FOREVER MY DOVE has been a labor of love, and a project in which I have presented my heart and soul. It is my sincere desire that this collection will stir heartfelt emotions, and that certain verses will make a connection of how you personalize friendship, love or being in love.

Ron Dailey
Author

My Sweet Angel

The smile that lights your little face has always been a special delight to me. I have watched you grow, and at times it has behooved me to keep you small and protected. I also know that one day, I will have to let you go.

You are and have always been a spiritual force in my life. Your existence has shaped me as a father, a person who desired to be a model for his little girl. I have not always done all the right things or made all the right choices, but when it came to you, I have made few compromises.

You have been an emotionally moving force in my life. You have gripped my imagination, my creativity, and given me the desire to become the very best writer I could possibly be. From your shaping and molding, I have now become an author.

Thanks for being my little girl!

Love,

Daddy

Neal Benge/Artist

Neal's unique style of watercolor has been described by many as being so lifelike that subjects seem to have a certain three dimensional feeling to them. Neal considers each feather a separate entity, a painting of itself. He believes that by taking detail far enough that it allows the viewer to actually feel the beauty of the painting.

It has been a blessing to have had the opportunity to work with another artist, one so talented, and inspiring. Our personalities have blended and complemented each other in such a way only to enhance every aspect of Forever My Dove.

I thank you Neal for your contribution to Forever My Dove, for your belief in me, and especially our very treasured friendship.

Ron Dailey

A Word Of Inspiration

DOVES ARE LIKE NO OTHER SPECIES known to mankind. When they mate, they mate forever, no matter how bad the circumstances or conditions they fly into, for they are lovebirds, truly in love, and very selective about their true love.

The expression, "Until Death Do We Part," is so true for these rare lovebirds, for as long as their truelove is alive, they will never consider the possibility of finding another mate.

Because of my fascination and fondness of doves, the following loveletters and letters of poetry are dedicated to Doves, the Lovebirds, and to those who genuinely seek Love.

First Meeting

As they gaze into each other's eyes, they feel the warmth of the sun as it rises. The fading away of a crescent moon tells White Feather and Sweetie Bird what time of day it is.

On this obscure branch deep in the Blue Ridge Mountains, there's a nervousness that hasn't been. Their nervousness is filled with excitement as they move closer during this first meeting.

It appears as though electricity is coming out of their beaks and sending a message that they can't deny. The night dissipates as day comes in. The lavender pink sky sets the stage for White Feather and Sweetie Bird to decide if they will be mates forever.

They move closer, and coo in unison. The amorous ritual has begun and a life long commitment has been made, and they will be by each other's sides for as long as they shall live.

Chemistry

Two strangers meet for the first time and realize there
is a certain chemistry kindling, and they
hunger for more.

There's no conversation at this point, only a feeling
deep inside that urges one to make the first move.

A warm hello is treated with a gracious smile
that indicates that it is all right to come closer,
and to say more.

This strange and wonderful energy that has ignited,
provides us with the unique capacity of knowing
what the other one is thinking before they do.

It's a strange phenomena, almost unexplainable,
a complexity of emotions that happens
between two.

In A Dove's Eye

Oh how they must wonder what that great night light is
in the sky, the light that brings inner peace, that tell them
it is time to settle down, and be still for the night.

Oh what a feeling it must ignite for the doves to witness the
moonlight as it glistens through the icicles bringing forth
light. Even as the moon comes up, the icicles must twinkle
and appear as diamonds as it reflects and twists before
reaching its final destination.

Even with all its wonder, beauty, and mystery, it really
doesn't matter, for all the dove really cares about is
being dry, having enough to eat, and having that spark
of love in his heart to see them through the night.

Home Away From Home

In a far away place, very deep in the Blue Ridge
Mountains, White Feather and Sweetie Bird make
their home in a nest left behind from another time.

They're content just to rub and nudge one another
and to share each other's heat to keep warm.

They comfort each other as the moon plays peek-a-boo
behind the evergreens. It's an icy night, very cold
outside; however, they seem not to notice or even care.

There's an inborn wisdom that creates a knowing that
they are inseparable. They are not only lovers, but they
are best friends. They will embark on a journey of true
love and sharing at its best.

Every year White Feather and Sweetie Bird will
come back to this home away from home, and if by
chance it is inhabited, they will find or built a
new home, without even making a fuss.

White Feather and Sweetie Bird have learned,
that home is not necessarily where one lays his
head, but where one chooses to lay his heart.

Captivated

Our short time relationship has inspired feelings I have never felt.
I want you to know I have been captivated by your sensitivity, your
soft approach, your openness, your outspokenness, your
intelligence, your persistence, your will,
and by far, your friendliness.

And it's fun just being with you

Do You Know

DO YOU KNOW how much I love you
Do you know how much I care

Do you know I'm thinking of you
Do you know you are my AIR

Do you feel the LOVE inside of me
Do you know it's always there

Do you know I'm thinking of you
Even when you're not here

Our Love

Love is a rare and precious gift. The GOOD LORD knew
this when he made doves. He knew that he could not
provide the gift to everyone, and was very
selective about his angelic doves.

We will fly the open blue sky. If you're hurting, I too
shall hurt, for I really do feel your intermost feelings.
I'm a part of you now and your feelings will always
be deeply felt and considered by me.

I have never loved another person with so much passion,
so much fever, and so much love. I have seen, felt,
and sensed parts of you no other man will ever see.
OUR LOVE can fulfill all of our needs.

I cannot explain to you all that I feel
There are no words that are that real

Under My Wing

It's cold outside
No place to go
Under my wing
Will Lift the snow

No food in sight
None on ground
Not even a sparrow
Flying around

I'll bring you birdseed
I hid away
Especially for you
On this snowy day

Under my wing
You just might find
A love that is endless
Without boundaries
Without time

Majestys Front Door

Majestically they flew
From Majesty's front door
With the message of love
For all to adore

God made them beautiful
Sprinkled with his love
Straight from heaven
Came the two doves

The moon lit the waters
And bestowed life upon a wing
Their love is so heavenly
So pure, so clean

Love straight from heaven
So obvious to see
As the two doves
Nestled on a hollow tree

Somewhere My Dove

I knew you before you walked into my life. I had always
wondered where you were, and then finally we met.
You're the person I had always thought about, that
special soulmate, the one who provides that glimmer,
that spark, and a tingly feeling all over.

Yes, I knew you before I had ever seen your face. You
are the person who can bring out the love that has
been sleeping in my wildest and purest dreams, the
one who brings inner strength.

I have dreamed about you a thousand times. Now,
you are here. At this magic moment, without you
knowing, I give you my heart, exposing myself
to you completely, because we are soulmates,
and meant to be.

In God's Time

After what seems like a lifetime
You have finally come along
I thought I had buried those feelings
And found out I was wrong

Your touch is like God's magic
It's all throughout the air
I can feel your presence
Even when you're not there

You know dreams are like magic
They're not always so true
But the magic I feel darling
Comes from loving you

It all now seems
To just fall in place
Why we never met
Until That Very Special Day

Special Power

You hold that special power
The power to make me feel whole
Or the power to make me feel incomplete

It's like the power that holds the stars above
Or the power that holds the earth beneath

It can be as sweet as a magnificent sunrise
Or as harsh as a stormy sea

You hold the Special Power, Darling
Capable of moving me

Someone Like You

There will never be someone like you in my life.
Someone I will always want to love just one more time.
Someone who, when I touch, I feel the love inside,
deep inside, begging for light, begging to feel
the magic of true love in the air.

Someone like you, someone like me, to feel the
true passions of love, of those that are truly in love.
Love at its highest peak, so sweet, so innocent, that it
is often mistaken for a heated affair.

There will never be someone like you in my life. I
give you my heart. I give you my love, and yes I desire
you, and yes I want to make love to you, and
Yes, It's From Above.

Yes, I Love You!

The Gift Of Love

Of all the people I have ever met, seen or really know, I have never met, seen or really known anyone so right for one another.

I love you so much and just saying so, sometimes frustrates me. At times it's difficult trying to express my feelings in the form of true love.

When you and I are actually touching and loving each other in such a way, then soft feelings become really apparent. When the love for one another takes precedence over everything else, then true love occurs at its best.

When I make love to you, I will put you first. I will care about your feelings and how you feel at the moment. I will love you like you have never been loved before, because I love you now more than you can ever be loved.

Love

LOVE IS A BEAUTIFUL WORD and for those who fall in love, there's almost a magnetic field around them that attracts the eyes for all others to see. LOVE creates an imagery in one's mind that makes one feel that they have been the chosen one, chosen to carry the dream of love forward, and perhaps to give hope to those who have never loved.

WHEN IN LOVE, one becomes a mirror, almost a reflection of what the other one is thinking. There seems to be a direct wave-length that permits the highest sensory communication between each other.

IN FACT, all of our sensory receptors seems to be very awake, and very stimulated. We want to make this significant one very happy. We want to shower them with gifts given from the heart. We want them to know they are the only one, the main event in our life.

FOR THOSE who fall in love, isn't it Wonderful to be in love, Mutually in love, and Forever in love.

Down And Under

Drawn by the sweet nectar of Gods
So enticing, only a Saint could say no
It provides only a small taste of its
honey to set the trap

Isn't it true in all walks of life--we are often attracted to things, in fact, lured in by special means, things aren't what they seem, and before we realize it, we are in over our head.

Once the honey has been sipped, the road back is never easy, and one that most often requires more endurance than one can stand. More often, it requires the love of a true friend.

Faithful Friend

When your load
Gets too heavy
And you have had
All that you can stand
Run to me, darling
I'm your faithful friend

I'll be there
When you need me
No matter what time you call
There's nothing I wouldn't do for you
No, nothing at all

The way I love you
Is far more than I can understand
One thing I do know for certain
Is that our friendship will never end

Grace Of A Dove

Through the sailing blue sky
Flies a bird in disguise
A gift from God
A dream come true
With the Grace of a Dove
She flies to you

She flies a particular pattern
To a nest she will call home
Flies to a true mate always known
Flies what she presently feels
Her new life full of thrills
They sail through the setting of the Sun

A Salted Tear

He spreads his wing
Under a starless night
She hovers beneath
Knowing no fright

He gathers her close
Close as can be
She senses his love
This awkward eve

An eternal tear
Crawls from her eye
He tastes salt`
And understands why

Center Of The Eye

Although Love comes from the Center of the Heart, the Flame of
Love has its' first spark from the Center of the Eye, that first look
where glorious feelings are unlocked. Those before feelings
that were black and blue, are now tossed aside
like a worn-out shoe.

In a small space in time, you are transcended to the Top of the
World, and the grounds beneath you shake on Mother Earth.
All this brought about by feelings of Love, feelings so strong,
it's difficult to put into words.

Those words that do appear seem to be hand-stitched from
God above, flown in specially on the Wings of a Dove. It all
started from that first look, the first look, from the
Center of the Eye.

Worn-out Shoe

From the Center of the Heart
Glorious feelings are unlocked
Feelings that were black and blue
Tossed aside like a worn-out shoe

Transcended to the top of the world
All because of a Special Girl
One look into the Center of the Eye
Sparks feelings you can't deny

Feelings hand-stitched from God above
Flown in by a Special Dove
Feelings that were black and blue
Tossed aside like a worn-out shoe

The Eye

We see with an eye, and it is the eye
we first see. If one looks closer, they will
see that the eye is a window that the heart
and mind leaks through.

Oh yes, the eye reveals all of your feelings.
This is the reason eye contact is diminished or
highlighted in our conversations. If one is on top
of the world, his eye contact with be spontaneous.

In fact, those eyes will grab you to ensure
they have your sole attention. On the other
hand, if one is feeling down, they look at
the ground, exposing their feelings for all to see.

Just look at the eyes, and you will see what
all generations have seen, "That the eye is an
extension of the heart, the mind, and the soul."

Open Season Day

Through the clouds
They emerge as one
Known as White Feather
And Sweetie Bird

They fly high
Then fly low
Through the treetops
They go

Over the peak
Around the bend
There's a closeness
That hasn't been

White Feather pigeoning in
On the ideal place to roost
Flies over a soybean patch
Trying to choose

With 100 guns aimed
Deadly at their hearts

White Feather senses a mistake
And darts to his left
And Sweetie Bird follows
With angelic grace

Escaping danger far below
Sweetie Bird coos amorously
With White Feather
On Open Season Day

Season's End

White Feather, can you ask for anything more?
You have had me perched on this limb since early dawn.
It makes it difficult when I know home is not that far away.
In fact, if we left right now, we could make it in a couple of days.

Now Sweetie Bird, you know I'm only thinking of you,
I've spotted three more hunters in camouflage suits.
I do not think it's going to last very long, several of those
hunters have already packed their guns and gone.

Earlier in the day, the racket and ear piercing noise was
all that they could stand, as they watched the lead
pellets multiply on the land.

The theater behind them undraped a spectacular red sky.
White Feather sensed it was time to make the decision or to
lay down and die. As they sprung from that limb and into
the crimson red sky, it became obvious that God had
provided a bulletproof guide.

As the last of the great hunters took sight on the two
doves, they flew right over them, protected by God's Love.

Teenage Love

As she told me about her feelings for a young boy
she had fallen for, I couldn't help but realizing
that these feelings had the potential to be powerful,
tragic, or wonderful in their own right.

Even at this tender age, emotions of love shoot
straight to the heart. Without having gained
the experience of surviving a relationship gone bad,
the breaking up of teenage love can be disastrous.

This can be a time when teens or pre-teens really
need someone to lean on, someone they can talk to,
someone to help explore these feelings and bring
them to the top, not to criticize, but to lift them up.

It is often a time to provide helpful information
in a subtle way, and to realize how our comments
can affect a young one's heart, and may possibly change
how they will perceive love today, as well as tomorrow.

These teen years are just as challenging for us
as parents, as it is for these teen hearts, and there
are no special formulas for us to adopt.

All we have in front of us is the child that we
dearly love, and we must handle this situation
delicately to foster a special trust.

A Pot Of Gold

An Arc of Spectral Colors
Appearing in the sky
Opposite the Sun
For You and I

Scientists say,
A result of
Refractive dispersion
Of light, rain, or mist

Others would have you believe,
A sign of the devil, darkness and despair.
A symbol which is celebrated at eh witches' fair

For those who have witnessed the beauty of
A rainbow after a short rainfall in June,
Know that it is only there for a few
Seconds and then it is gone

Leaving behind only its memory,
And possibly an illusion of hope

And for those who have stared
At its radiant beauty realize
Fully that this is God's work

You Were On My Mind

There's no reason to check my heart
I know exactly how I feel
It's like I've been away forever
Not just through the foothills

I recall you on my mind the day I left
And you were on my mind the day I came home
You were with me in the valleys, the hills,
The canyons, and the beautiful mountains I roamed

I thought about you during each sunset
And I thought about you during each dawn
I pulled the covers gently around me
And I wished I was at home

You were on my mind the day I left
And you were on my mind the day I came home
Not just through the valleys
But all the ground I roamed

Love Song

I overheard two lovers expressing a familiar love song
A tune which brought them together only weeks before

This song was so sweet and pure
One which would pierce the heart forever more
It was so sweet to listen to, and so nice to hear

The look in these lover's eyes was full of joy
They seemed to stare deeply and reflected every care

One lover had two doves on his shirt
The second lover had them on her coffee mug
It was so obvious they were in LOVE

I overheard two lovers expressing a familiar love song
A tune which brought them together only weeks before

Shelter From The Storm

The storm has moved in without warning. It has come with brilliant flashes of white light, and sounds of thunder that can be heard throughout the night. The mighty winds bring the rain and leave a supernatural feeling all over.

There's no place to go and certainly no place to hide. White Feather and Sweetie Bird find refuge under an old hollow tree. All they have is each other to weather the storm.

Isn't this an interesting principle? When times in your own personal life are so bad, where do you go, where do you run?

Do you have someone to weather the storm, or does the storm weather you? It's very important for someone to be there with open arms; that someone is your shelter, Shelter From The Storm.

Just Naturally

There's a relaxation between us that is so rare, so unique,
that I feel only a few people in THIS WORLD will ever know
I can expose myself to you completely, knowing you
are only going to Love Me More

I am IN LOVE with our relationship, our conversations, and
totally in love with you. When I'm with you, there's nothing
else, Nothing Else More Special than you

You're everything to me, and I want you to feel Special,
because that's what I feel, truly feel. I have given up all
those hang-ups, knocked down all those walls,
I'm letting it happen, Just Naturally

One Look

All of your life
You dream of that special one
Someone to share in everything
Your best friend, indeed

Then one day
There they are
That first look
That's all it took

You're different now
Transformed into a new person
One look
Is all it took

You'll never be the same again
And all it took
Was One Look
One Very Special Look

In Love

I know
You feel
I think
We are

You know
I feel
You think
We are

We know
We feel
We think
We are

She's There

I see her face
Wherever I go
I close my eyes
She's there I know

Her dark brown hair
Blowing in the wind
Her gracious smile
Again and again

The magnetism of her eyes
Stops me at my feet
Gives me strength
Beyond belief

I see her face
Wherever I go
She's in my mind
This I know

My Darling

My Love

My Sweetness

My Dove

Shooting Star

She flew to me
Like a shooting star
I had all …..
But quit looking
And there she was

FIRST LOOK
FIRST TOUCH
FIRST KISS

Were unquestionable
Unbelievable

Something about her eyes
Seemed to reveal
My very soul

Exposed feelings
I just didn't know

She flew to me
Like a shooting star
I had all …..
But quit looking
And there we were

White Dove

Morning glories, how are you
As you dance around my nest
Your flowers are a blooming
And you're looking your best

You may not know it
But, I've been around
Since the beginning of time
Even sailed with Noah
When no land could be found

I have been used
As a peace symbol
During times of distress
Often used in weddings
To represent the best

Proud to be a white dove
So different from the rest
With a message of love
For all of God's best

Falling For You

Since the first time I laid eyes on you I instantly knew.
You were everything I had looked for my entire life. When
you finally showed up on the scene, I had all, but
quit looking, and there you were.

Right from the start, the attraction was
so mutual, and we both knew we were falling for
each other. When we looked into each other's eyes, it
was obvious that there was something more, something
never quite felt before.

Yet, it has happened so quickly. At times, I want to step
back, step back to absorb it all, but my heart hungers
for more. I cannot step back, I just do not want to.

I am hopelessly falling for you!!!

More Than Friends

I love you so deeply
So thoroughly it hurts
I long to be with you
To feel your touch

I hurt when you're not around
I hurt when we can't talk
I hurt when we can't touch
I'm just hurt, hurt, hurt

Do you hurt and long for me
As I hurt, hurt for you
Do you feel the pain
When our love is restrained

Do you know
Where we are going
Do you know
Where we have been

I love you so much Darling
More than just friends

Until I Met You

Never felt the passion of true love in the air
Couldn't experience true love
Because you were not there

The way you touch when I need a hand
An encouraging word from my best friend

Never dreamed true love could be like this
Felt to the marrow
And nothing but bliss

Yes, things have changed
Since I met you
Even the gray skies
Now turn blue

The Way You Love Me

I know you love me
I can feel it in your eyes

The way you hold me
It's no surprise

The things you say
On an ordinary walk

The touching of hands
When we talk

No, it's not the same
With anybody else

The way you love me
Is beyond the best

Romance

JUST AS THE SUN wakes up the sleeping petals of a rose,
and they flower open to feel its glow, romance creates
a similar stage whereas the hearts blossom outwardly,
and sensational feelings begin to explode

ROMANCE is the substance that love fulfilling and
long lasting relationships are fastened from. It is
as much a part of love, as sculpturing and drawing
is a part of art.

SOMEWHERE deep inside, comments like, "You make
me happier than I have ever been", are still waiting
to be heard, but are usually left behind. When
feelings of love are not expressed, we are often
left alone, only to worry and guess.

ROMANCE is a work of art, and a lifetime commitment
that should occur daily in the way we treat
and think of the one we love. Being romantic
to the one you love takes so little time,
and the return is OFTEN tenfold.

WHAT each of us needs now, is romance, sweet romance,
it's the only thing, to keep our true love alive.

He Rules His Nest With An Iron Claw, Or Does He?

Sweetheart, it's time to take a shower.
Okay daddy, I just wanted to finish my cola.

Son, I want you in bed in a few minutes.
Yes sir dad, I am on my way.

Sweetheart, have you taken that shower yet?
I will daddy in a few minutes.

Son, I do not want to have this discussion with you again.
Now go to bed!
Yes sir dad, goodnight!

Sweetheart, what are you doing up?
Daddy, I have to have pleats in these pants for tomorrow.
I have nothings else to wear. Sweetheart, you better
get into bed, or we are going to pleat something else.
Okay daddy, I will wear something dirty. Now sweetheart,
you have other clean clothes to wear, now go to bed.
I do not want to have to tell you to go to bed again tonight.

Son, did I not just tell you to go to bed? Yes sir dad, but I just
wanted to see why sweetheart was up.

On A Summer's Day

The way we fell in love
Is so unique to me
Met you on a summer's day
In the middle of June

Your eyes were sparkling
As I looked at you that day
A smile belonging to an angel's face

Your dark brown hair
Was as pretty as could be
The smell of roses
Made me weak in my knees

One look at you
Was all I could stand
For those very first few minutes
Were the best I ever had

Our Cup

I'm so much in love with you
That my cup runneth over into your cup
Your cup becomes my cup
My cup becomes your cup
Our Cup becomes **The Cup**

My feelings are your feelings
Your feelings are my feelings
Love is our feeling
If we are considerate of those feelings
We feel just fine

God's Messenger

There was an old lady who had lost her dear son.
She wondered if he would go to heaven,
or be lost in his own sin.

The sweet old lady prayed diligently the same
prayer from dusk until dawn; she wondered
if the Good Lord would take her boy home.

Then one morning at the crack of day, this sweet
old lady gazed at her windowsill and
was truly amazed. There in all its beauty
was a white dove, glaring deeply as
though in disguise.

This sweet old lady instantly knew that
this was a sign from God above, because God
often sends meaningful messages on
The Wings of a White Dove

God's Promise

God saw the wickedness of the earth
And made a decision to destroy it
Because Noah had the straight walk and the straight talk
The Lord spared Noah and his wife and his three sons and their wives

And instructed Noah to build an ark,
A vessel big enough for all who wanted to be saved
The people around thought Noah was out of his mind
And not one would climb on board
The Lord instructed Noah to gather 2 of every creature of every kind
And to build a room for thee
So for forty days and forty nights
The Lord flooded the earth with waters
And every living creatures on earth and in the air was destroyed
And even the tallest mountains were covered with waters
And no land could be found

Noah stretched out his hand
And released two birds, first a raven, and then a white dove
The raven did not return, but the white dove did, without signs of land
Noah waited a week to let the waters rescind
And Noah sent the white dove out again
And like magic, the white dove appeared with an olive branch
Giving proof that the land was near
And a rainbow appeared over Noah's ark
The same rainbow you see every now and then
The rainbow is God's Promise to every living creature
That he will never flood the earth with the waters again

Lighthouse

Sailing along
Looking for home
Out of darkness
A way was shown

A beacon of light
Came to me
The light of Jesus
Set me free

What was dark
Now became white
The love of Jesus
Gave me peace

Tucked in his love
Safe to keep
Since his light
Has set me free

Friends

Every now and then
You need a friend
One you can count on
No matter when

One who's there
Through thick and thin
Always in the background
Wishing you to win

One who seems to understand
In all you do and say
A joy to be with
From day to day

A true friend
Is so different from the rest
They care about your feelings
And wish you the best

It just so happens
That most people you know
Call themselves your friend
But haven't a clue

Chain Of Love

THERE IS A LINK between two when they fall in love. This link is made of gold that crosses over an imaginary space. This space which was once titled private or personal space now allows your entry. You have now been given the key, much like being given the key to the city, but this is of greater consequence, this is the key to the heart.

THE KEY to the heart opens and shuts all doors. It is with this key that one may become motivated to heights beyond imagination. Feelings never explored before now make their way known. There is a link in this Chain of Love that is solid gold, a bond so strong, appearing impossible to grow old. This link is often referred to as BEING IN LOVE.

FEELINGS of affection and of mutual trust are now displayed in every way. The bond of lasting love will be reflected from day to day. It is from this bond that true love grabs its roots, and imaginary love soon fades away.

LOVE is as much as an art as can possibly be. It has many golden links and connections, in which all fit into the CHAIN OF LOVE.

On A Cloud

a kiss   a kiss
kiss   kiss   kiss   kiss   kiss   kiss
I   have   been   on   a   cloud   since   I   met
you   the   other   day.   The   very   first   words
you   said to me still linger, and   when you   asked   me to
sit with you,   my   heart   skipped   a   beat.   I   was   beside
myself,   lost   in time   for   a   few   moments, and   all   I   could
do   was   fall   into   the   seat   beside   you.   And   when   your   leg
touched   mine   while   sitting,   although   I   thought   it   was
accidental,   it   took   my   breath   away.   I   haven't   been
the   same   since.   All   I   know   is   that I   must   see   you
again.   I   feel   as   though I   have   always   known
you,   and although it is true, we only   spent   one
hour   together,   those   were   the   most   fabulous
60 minutes I had   ever   spent   with   anyone.
Yes,   I   have   been   on   a   cloud,
since   I   saw   you   last.
I   can't   wait
to   see   you
again
.

74

Dreams Do Come True

I recall the first time I saw her, her eyes were more intoxicating
than wine. It was as though, in another time, our spirits
had kissed, mingled, and danced like shadows on
the outskirts of a huge rainforest

Our souls had touched, in such a way, that we knew, there
was no going back, there was no Return to Yesterday

Our eyes, our touch, our spirits, are all a part of what has
become magic, total magic, and capable of Moving the Sun

As we venture forward, we realize that dreams do come true,
and that love is not just something one reads about.
or sees in the movies. Love happens!

Forever My Dove

You know poetry and words of rhythm are nice to listen to
And they make you feel so good
But sometimes it's difficult to express love
In a riddle or a word or two

So I want you to know that you're everything to me
And I have only known you for such a short while
There is something so deep, from the essence of my very soul
That instructs me on this very day to say
"YOU are my darling, you are my life,
You are my sweetheart, and soon to be my wife"

WE have a DREAM most people can never find
Something REAL Something DIVINE
On this day I ask of you to share in this DREAM
To LOVE me forever as I will LOVE you
To become a part of my soul, my heart too

I ask you to accept this ring
As a SYMBOL of our LOVE
And to remember us always
As flying DOVES

I will love you forever with all of my heart
Will you marry me SWEET DARLING
And become my SWEET WIFE

The First Born

Even before their young is born, they share turns in laying on the egg, usually the father by day, and the mother by night, so she can be watchful and protect her family, while her truelove sleeps.

During the day, the mother will gently nudge the father off of the egg, so he can go and get food and water. When he returns minutes later, she gets off of the egg, and allows him to sit on the egg until night falls.

When all this responsibility seems to be more than they can endure, the male dove is often spotted with his wing stretched over his truelove keeping her warm and full of joy.

It is a sight to behold to observe these two lovebirds in action. They play together and share in responsibilities related to parenting. The male dove also produces crop milk to feed the young.

In closing, the dove has always stood for something else. The dove has been a symbol for the Holy Ghost, a symbol in Noah's adventures, and a symbol used throughout peacetime negotiations. However, probably more than anything else, the dove has become the symbol of love.

It is this association that has guided my feelings, and my writings in Forever My Dove. One only has to be around doves for a few minutes to see their amorous qualities and to understand how they have earned this symbol throughout the world.

About the Author

This is the 2nd edition of Forever My Dove, a unique collection of love poems. The 1st edition was published in 1995 and due to popularity is now being released again. Crossing all genres, Ron has written the following novels: You Have the Right to Remain Silent, a Detective Suspense; Pockets of Love, a WW11 Romance; Rattlesnake Suspenders, a mind-bending Time Travel/Romance; A Doll Without a Face, a Detective Thriller; and Black Moon, a Romance Thriller. He also writes poetry in all his novels, and You Have the Right to Remain Silent has just been released. His other novels are sure to follow.

Ron Dailey has an Associate in Arts Degree, Bachelor of Science Degree in Psychology, Graduate Work in Psychology and Certified at the Master Level in Psychology by DHR, Master of Science Degree in Administration, and an Associate of Science Degree in Nursing. His past work experiences include being a Training Center Psychologist/Behavior Specialist, a Director of a Mental Retardation Program, and a Therapist in Emergency Rooms. He also worked as a Production Manager at Robins Air Force Base. Ron is the owner and President of Lighthouse Nursing Agency, a staffing company, and is all over the state of Georgia.

About the Artist

Neal Benge has 20 years' experience in wildlife and graphics arts. He has twice been a finalist in the national competition of the Federal Duck Stamp Contest. His work has been featured on the front cover of the Waterfowl USA magazine, the Macon magazine, and the 1995 Economic Impact of Warner Robins AFB, in Georgia. Neal painted all the artwork in Forever My Dove, and Ron Dailey states their relationship was magical during the production of Forever My Dove.

Neal is married to his wife, Glenda, has two daughters, Allyson and Julie, and one son, Clint.